First published in Belgium and Holland by Clavis Uitgeverij, Hasselt – Amsterdam, 2017
Copyright © 2017, Clavis Uitgeverij

English translation from the Dutch by Clavis Publishing Inc. New York
Copyright © 2018 for the English language edition: Clavis Publishing Inc. New York

Visit us on the web at www.clavisbooks.com

Doctors and What They Do (small size edition) written and illustrated by Liesbet Slegers
Original title: *De dokter*
Translated from the Dutch by Clavis Publishing

ISBN 978-1-60537-386-7

This book was printed in June 2017 at Poligrafia Janusz Nowak Spólka z o.o.,
62-081 Wysogotowo, ul. Zbozowa 7, Poland

First Edition
10 9 8 7 6 5 4 3 2 1

Clavis Publishing supports the First Amendment and celebrates the right to read

Doctors
and What They Do
Liesbet Slegers

Clavis

NEW YORK

Doctors tell you how to stay healthy and fit.
They know all about the body.
If you're sick, they figure out what's wrong.
The doctor knows how to make you better
and what medicines you need.

hello!

The doctor wears a white coat over her regular clothes. She takes her doctor's bag with her on house calls. A doctor who performs surgeries is covered from head to toe!

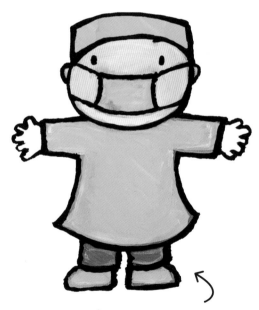

ready for an operation

long white coat

doctor's bag

The doctor examines you on the exam table.
She has everything she needs—even a stethoscope.
She uses other instruments to treat you,
like tweezers and a bandage.

the doctor records
everything on
the computer

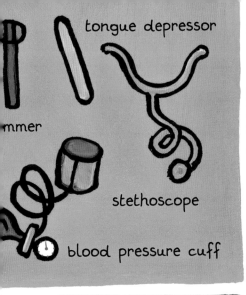

tongue depressor

mmer

stethoscope

blood pressure cuff

plastic gloves

syringe

light

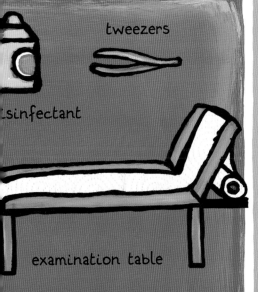

tweezers

:sinfectant

examination table

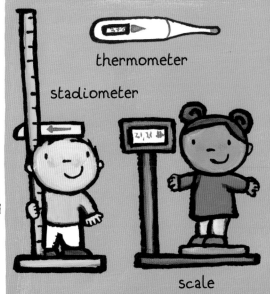

thermometer

stadiometer

scale

"Hi, Liam! How are you?" asks the doctor.

"I have an earache," sighs Liam.

"Liam also has a fever and a bad cough," says Daddy.

waiting in the waiting room

The doctor listens to Liam's lungs with a stethoscope. "I can hear your heartbeat. What a beautiful sound," says the doctor. "Take a deep breath, Liam."

looking inside the ears

"Now I'm going to feel your belly,"
says the doctor. "How does that feel?
Open your mouth. Then I can look at your throat.
Good! All done."

looking at the throat

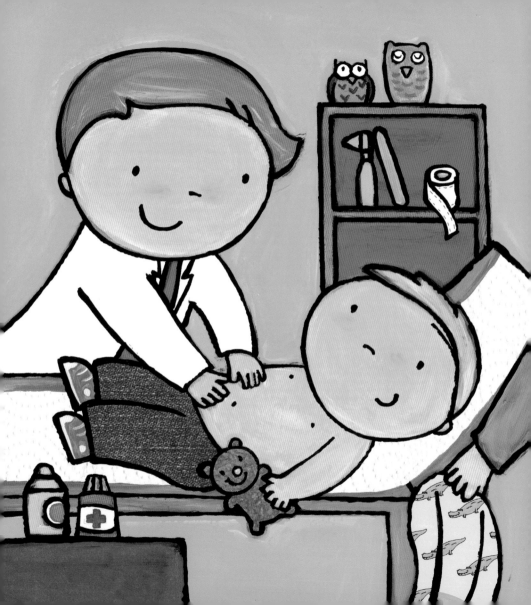

"You must stay home from school for a few days,
so that you can rest," says the doctor.
"I'll prescribe some medicine for you."
"We'll get it at the pharmacy," says Daddy.

thank you, doctor!

The next patient is a baby.
She isn't sick but needs a shot
to protect her against diseases.
Well done!

vaccination book

Now the doctor has to go to the emergency room. Patients go there when they need help right away. It's very busy here! Do you see the ambulance?

beep, beep!

"So, my dear, what happened?" asks the doctor. Lola is crying. "I fell off my bike," she says. "My arm really hurts!"

The nurse takes a special photo of the inside
of Lola's arm.
The doctor can see it on the computer.
"I see. There's a crack in the bone,"
says the doctor.

Lola gets a cast on her arm.
"It can come off in a few weeks," says the doctor.
Lola smiles.
When children go home happy,
the doctor is happy too.

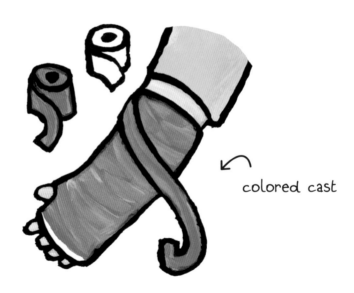

colored cast

A doctor can be a family doctor,
but can do other things too!

Some doctors perform surgeries
with the help of nurses.

There are doctors who know
all about babies in their
mommy's tummies.